SNAP OUT OF IT?

A QUICK GUIDE TO
OVERCOMING PANIC AND ANXIETY

SNAP OUT OF IT?

A QUICK GUIDE TO
OVERCOMING PANIC AND ANXIETY

BY JUDSON ROTHSCHILD

ISBN 10: 1453802924
ISBN 13: 9781453802922

PRAISE FOR JUDSON ROTHSCHILD

"Judson Rothschild has written the ideal book for those struggling with the often-crippling impact of anxiety and panic attacks. He combines his own experience with well-researched material. Judson writes with clarity, humor and purpose, seeking to share his own hard-earned wisdom with others in search of real-life answers. Those looking for hope and help will not be disappointed."

—RICK SHUMAN, PhD, vice chair, Our House
Past clinical director, Century City Hospital
Frequent guest on CNN, CBS, FOX, OPRAH and EXTRA

"This is the perfect book to give to people suffering from panic and/or anxiety. It delivers exactly what it promises: quick, useful, medically sound advice that gives patients hope, while helping them become advocates in their own recovery."

—DR. ROBERT GERNER, M.D., Psychiatrist
Associate research psychiatrist, UCLA School of Medicine
Founder, Affective Disorder Clinic, UCLA
President, Pacific Institute for Medical Research

"*Snap Out of It?* is a courageous, optimistic, spiritual book from Judson Rothschild's heart, using as a guide his own life experiences, from which we all have much to learn."

—DAVID R. ALLEN, M.D.
Leader in alternative and complementary medicine
Los Angeles, California

"This book is a transformational journey into the depths of panic and anxiety and is a clear and comprehensive practical guide for transcendence. A most useful tool for finding peace and spirituality. Judson's enlightened journey unlocks the love, wisdom and power found in one's own deep inner soul."

—GARY QUINN, bestselling author
Living In the Spiritual Zone

"*Snap Out of It?* is packed with straightforward, essential strategies for effectively dealing with panic and/or anxiety, leaving the reader inspired and empowered."

—DEBBIE FORD, *New York Times* bestselling author
Dark Side of the Light Chasers and
Why Good People Do Bad Things

"The true test of character is defined
by how we deal with the unexpected."
—*Judson Alan Rothschild*

CONTENTS

FOREWORD

"**W**hat makes you think you're qualified to write a book on panic and anxiety? You're not a doctor or a medical expert. Why is anyone going to want to buy your book?"

My answer to these questions is simple.

I possess one thing that most of these doctors and medical experts do not. I have personally survived twenty years of panic and anxiety, and I'm still standing. And believe me when I say it, I've earned the equivalent of a master's degree!

Some wonderful books on panic and anxiety have been written by medical experts. I am not attempting to compete with them. You will not find case studies in this book, nor will you read hundreds of pages of dedicated, documented research material.

Snap Out of It! A Quick Guide to Panic and Anxiety is exactly that. A quick guide. When you are in the throes of panic and/ or anxiety, you need easy access to useful information, and you want it fast. The sheer thought of looking at a four-hundred-page medical book is daunting even when you are not having these problems.

Over the years, I have read hundreds of medical and self-help books. In the last few years, I have discovered an alarming trend. If you use a highlighter when you read these books and look back when you are finished, you will discover only ten to twenty pages have truly given you insight. The other three hundred-plus have been nothing but filler.

My concept for this book is very simple: to give the reader as much information as I can in fewer than one hundred and twenty pages, thus making it easier to start applying the tools right now. TODAY.

Chapter One

IS THERE A DOCTOR IN THE HOUSE?

"Doctor, doctor, give me the news,
I've got a bad case of lovin' you!"
—*John Moon Martin*

It is unfair to your friends and loved ones to have to shoulder the responsibility for dealing with your symptoms. Odds are pretty good that they are as exhausted by this process as you are. I recommend that you start by getting a thorough physical examination from your general practitioner. If your doctor determines that you have no physical medical issues, I suggest finding a mental health practitioner who specializes in panic and anxiety. This book is not meant to take the place of medical experts; it is to be used in conjunction with them.

Remember that your doctor or therapist cannot read your mind. You must take a proactive role in reclaiming your life. At the end of this book, you will find a RECIPE FOR PANIC AND ANXIETY. Fill it out carefully. Discuss your symptoms with your doctor, and do not be afraid to tell him or her how panic and anxiety have affected any or all areas of your life. If you feel your doctor does not have a good sense of your issues, or for some reason you do not connect well, find another one. You need to have someone whom you feel you can trust. You have been battling this issue for way too long. A good therapist can give you the assurances you need and provide you with the proper tools to slay this panic and anxiety dragon forever. You are not alone in this quest. The sooner you realize this, the faster you will gain relief.

Chapter Two

SNAP OUT OF IT?

*(If you are currently experiencing panic and/or anxiety,
go straight to Chapter Three)*

For those of you lucky enough never to have experienced panic and anxiety, trust me when I say this is something you would not wish on your worst enemy!

Imagine a large hand coming down from the sky, entering your body through the top of your head, and pushing all hope and positive feelings out of your body and soul. You are left with nothing but gloom and doom. Suddenly your body reacts as if you have stepped off the curb in front of an oncoming car. The scary thing is, there is no curb, nor is there a car. You are actually sitting in your chair at your office. You look around like a wild person. You must be going crazy. If feeling crazy is not bad enough, your body retaliates. You break out in a sweat. Every muscle in your body screams, "Run!"

You have no idea what is happening to you. It feels as if you have jumped out of your skin! The world is upside down. A feeling of unreality starts drifting in, and then the anxiety. Oh, no! Not that feeling again! Panicked, you start climbing back into your skin as quickly as you can. Anything to stop that feeling! You push, you stretch, you shove, and you desperately suck in your breath every inch of the way, finally managing to pull up that zipper over your skin.

You can barely breathe. There is not one ounce of your body that does not feel as if it is going to claw, tear and rip itself right out of your skin. You are so uncomfortable, you cannot imagine feeling like this for another second, let alone another minute. Ten minutes?! Oh, my God! The thought of an hour feeling like this? You decide right then that you will kill yourself! What? Where did that thought come from? Oh, my God, you are going crazy! At that moment, you want to tear every ounce of skin off your body and run down the street, screaming, "Help me! Please help me! Please! God, someone help me!"

But guess what? You are not running down the street. You are still in your office.

You look around, panicked. You start calling your friends and loved ones. Beads of sweat appear on your forehead. Your armpits are soaked. You tell your friends, family and loved ones that you are feeling strange, that you want to jump out of your skin. The more you try to put the feeling into words, the worse the effects. Without knowing it, you have started to hold your breath.

After listening to you, your friends and loved ones offer many inspirational responses:

"YOU THINK YOU ARE HAVING A BAD DAY? YOU WANT TO KNOW WHAT HAPPENED TO ME?"

"GET A GRIP."

"HONEY, I REALLY DON'T HAVE TIME FOR THIS. I'M LATE PICKING UP THE DOG FROM THE GROOMER'S."

Or the all-time-best one…

"SNAP OUT OF IT!"

Your worst fear has come true.

You hang up the phone. There is no denying it. You are

all alone! You sit there, shaking, re-evaluating your whole life, which is flashing in front of you like a Warner Brothers B movie.

Just this morning, you felt as if you were on top of the world. You have a great job, a great life. Soon, you are going on an incredible two-week vacation to Paris.

Now, you are nothing but a quivering mess. How did this happen?

Snap out of it? You still cannot believe your ears. If you could frickin' snap out of this, why would you have called anybody? The tears start as your body uncontrollably rumbles and twitches. Overwhelming sadness shakes you to your soul. You truly feel as if you are in this all alone.

Chapter Three

PANIC OR ANXIETY?

"Whatever the mind can conceive and believe,
the mind can achieve."
—*Napoleon Hill*

First, let me start by reminding you that stupid people do not have panic and/or anxiety. Research has shown that it takes a highly intelligent, creative brain to conjure invisible monsters. So it is important to remind yourself that there is a plus side: You have a great creative brain and an extremely high IQ. Soon, you will learn how to use that creative IQ to slay the invisible monsters and create a life of abundance and hope. And the good news is…it's not that far away.

There is a fine line between panic and anxiety. I have read many books on the subject, and quite frankly, I was more confused after reading them than I was when I started. Some argue that anxiety comes first and panic follows. Others say just the opposite. Personally, I really did not care which came first.

Didn't these people understand? I was in the middle of having an attack. I just wanted it to STOP! I didn't want a dissertation. I wanted answers.

I have spent enough money on this panic vs. anxiety issue to be quite sure I've put many therapists' children through college. I'm not going to spend time debating the books and the medical experts here, because, in fact, I cannot. I am not a doctor, nor do I have any informal medical training, for that matter. I do, however, possess one thing most of these doctors probably do not. To date, I have personally survived two decades of panic and anxiety. And as I have stated before—believe me when I say it—I have earned my degree!

The start of my panic and anxiety journey was a true revelation. To my horror, I discovered there was no clinic or specialist for these specific issues. The year was 1988, and at the time there were two options: medication and/or hospitalization.

I had never had a drink, nor had I ever smoked, taken drugs or had a cup of coffee: I grew up seeing too much abuse of these substances. Therefore, medication did not seem the right option to me. (We will discuss the pros and cons of medication in a later chapter.) Hospitalization posed even more problems, including cost and time. These concerns only fed the anxiety. Not to mention the fact that you are placed in a ward with people who have severe psychiatric issues. That is the *last* place someone who is feeling panic and anxiety needs to be. You already fear that you are going crazy (which, of course, you are not; we will discuss this in a later chapter as well). Why would anyone think a hospital was the appropriate place for someone suffering from panic and anxiety?

I found myself asking many questions, and no one had any answers. And I discovered a discord between the psychiatric community and the psychological community: The psychiatric community felt that medication was the answer, while the psychological community felt that talking through your issues was what was needed. After months of no sleep and constantly wanting to jump out of my skin, it did not take a flash of genius to figure out that there had to be a happy medium.

What follows are the benefits/results/lessons/knowledge gleaned from two decades of personal research. From this point on, it is imperative to view yourself as a RESEARCHER, not as a victim. Once you understand the physical and emotional responses to panic and anxiety, you will be able to say, "Oh, this is interesting. What did I just hear, say or feel that brought on that response?" "What was I telling myself in that moment?" "So that's why my body is sweating and twitching." "So I'm not going crazy."

No! You are not going crazy.

You just feel as if you are. Stop telling yourself that you are going crazy. We all do it. It just makes things worse. Your mind and body perceive the words "I am going crazy" *as a threat*, and *will respond* accordingly, which keeps the whole vicious cycle going. You are not going crazy: It truly is that simple. Now, let's get started on stopping that negative voice.

It is my experience and belief that anxiety is the precursor to panic, which is why we will deal with anxiety first.

We have all experienced anxiety at one time or another: walking down a dark street, on a bumpy plane ride, taking an important test, speaking in front of a group of people, waking from a bad dream in the middle of the night, hearing a sudden loud noise. Your response to these situations can vary from mild uneasiness to terror and panic. No matter what the response is, your body is doing exactly what it needs to do in order to survive. This reaction is known as the *fight or flight* response. This response is not harmful; your body is actually doing you a favor. It is protecting you and saving your life. The feelings of anxiety associated with the *fight or flight* response vary. They can last a brief moment, all day and night, quite possibly even a few days. But they are healthy, positive responses to the situation.

Remember, you are the RESEARCHER. Understand that your body is protecting you! YOU ARE FINE. THERE IS NOTHING WRONG WITH YOUR BODY. IT IS WORKING MAGNIFICENTLY, DOING EXACTLY WHAT IT SHOULD BE DOING!

Now that you realize that you are the RESEARCHER, gathering information, let us stop for a second and talk about the physiological signs that may accompany anxiety: edginess, irritability, breathlessness, fatigue, restlessness, difficulty sleeping, extreme muscle tension, choking, dizziness, spots before or blurring of the eyes, numbness and/or tingling, gastrointestinal discomfort and/or diarrhea, sweating, strange body odor. The list goes on and on.

It is important to remember that none of the mental or physical responses is harmful or dangerous. So why does all of this happen? That brings us back to the *fight or flight* response.

Anxiety is a response to danger and/or threat. Immediate or short-term anxiety comes from the *fight or flight* response. Depending on the danger, you will fight or you will run. Let us say you are walking down the street next to a construction site, and a huge crane starts to tip over. Workmen are screaming and yelling for everyone to "look out!" If you felt no anxiety, the odds are pretty good that you would be crushed and killed. Instead, the *fight or flight* response kicks in, and you run like hell to get out of the way.

As the RESEARCHER, what does this tell you? It tells you that nature has created anxiety as a way of protecting you, not of harming you. Anxiety is not dangerous. You just perceive it as dangerous. When you sit and worry about losing your job, what you are really telling your mind and body is "A crane is falling!" What happens? Your body starts responding. Thus the cycle begins. The physiological responses kick in: You start sweating, your left eye twitches, you can't seem to breathe, your body starts to tingle, and suddenly you are on your way to a wonderful anxiety attack.

But guess what? You are not losing your job. Your boss loves you. You are just worried about what would happen if you *did* lose your job. Meanwhile, look at what just showed up: DOOM AND GLOOM, your two best friends. Well, haven't you had enough of them? Let me show you how to get rid of them.

Chapter Four

WHY AM I SWEATING THE SMALL STUFF?

"Activity and sadness are incompatible."
—Christian Bovee

That is a very good question. But before I answer it, let us discuss why you are sweating.

It takes three systems to create anxiety:

1. **The Physical System** (which is really why you are sweating) provides all of the physical symptoms. If you are reading this book, you probably have experienced many of the following: tremors, muscle tension, hot flashes, chills, twitching, dizziness, breathlessness, rapid heartbeat, headaches, backaches, fatigue, insomnia, upset stomach, frequent urination, diarrhea, clammy hands and/or feet, chest pain…(And you thought you were all alone in this!)

2. **The Mental System** (our worst critic) provides those highly entertaining negative feelings. You should recognize these: "I am going crazy." "I am having a heart attack." "I have a brain tumor." "I am going to pass out." "There is something seriously wrong with me." Or my own personal favorite, "I am going to end up living under the freeway in a Sear's Kenmore Appliance box!" On top of these is the Cognitive Symptoms bonus, which includes inability to think clearly, anxious or racing thoughts, constant worrying, loss of memory, fearful

anticipation, poor judgment, etc. Last but not least...

3. **The Behavioral System** (to pace or not to pace). This is when our body takes action: pacing, nail biting, teeth grinding, overreacting, eating more or less, isolating, overdoing activities, sleeping too much or too little, etc.

It is safe to say that we have all experienced many or all of the symptoms listed above. As the RESEARCHER, you have to ask yourself why.

The answer may surprise you.

Are you ready? It is because you are healthy. You are normal. Your body is doing exactly what it is supposed to be doing. There is nothing wrong with your body.

"Then why am I feeling as if I am going crazy, and that my body is turning against me?" you ask.

Remember the falling crane analogy? Your negativity has become so insidious that, without being aware of it, you have told yourself multiple times during the day the equivalent of THE CRANE IS FALLING! "I'm not being paid enough; how am I going to pay my bills?" "I'm never going to make that deadline!" "I hate my boss!" "I'm going to lose my job." "I can't keep up with my work." "I can't keep up with the kids." "Why is my heart beating so fast?" "I'm having a heart attack." "I'm all alone." "I'm getting too old, and no one wants me." "What's going to happen if something happens to me?" "Where will I go?" "What will I do?" "Who will take care of me?" "Why is the engine of the plane slowing down?" "I can't get in that elevator; there are too many people." "I will go crazy and start screaming, and then I am going to pass out!" "Why am I sweating?" "I have to be in the aisle seat!" "I am late! They are going to kill me!" "I am going to lose it in this traffic!" "How am I going to get everything on my list done today?" "I am not speaking to her! I am never going to speak to her again, not after the way she treated me!" "How can I take care of everyone else when I can't take care of myself?"

The negativity list goes on and on. Do any of these ring a bell?

When you think any of these statements, you are telling your body, "THE CRANE IS FALLING," and your healthy body shifts into high gear, racing you toward the fight or flight response, protecting you from your demons.

As the RESEARCHER, you have already learned that, once the anxiety/panic button is pushed, your physical sensations can last anywhere from minutes to days. Therefore, your goal is simple: to learn to stop the negativity before it begins. One of the single most important things you will learn in this book is this: IT IS ABSOLUTELY IMPOSSIBLE TO HAVE ANXIETY OR PANIC IF YOU ARE RELAXED!

What? Yes, it is true. Here it is again: **IT IS ABSOLUTELY IMPOSSIBLE TO HAVE ANXIETY OR PANIC IF YOU ARE RELAXED!**

What does that tell you? It tells you that your job is to learn HOW TO RELAX. This book will teach you many ways to accomplish this, and the first will be to comprehend exactly what your body is doing during the *fight or flight* response. Once you understand this, you will be able to spot the signs as they happen, and with the tools you will learn here, you will be able to slay the panic and anxiety dragons, and live the peaceful life you deserve.

Chapter Five

UNDERSTANDING THE WILD BEAST

"The best way to see Faith is to shut the eye of Reason."
—*Benjamin Franklin*

When you are under stress, the *fight or flight* response kicks in. So what is stress? Stress is a psychological and physiological response to events that occur in your life. There are many types of stress: daily hassles and demands, major life events and, most important in panic and anxiety, the internal critical voice.

Research has shown that you can take the most well-adjusted person and put him or her under prolonged stress, and eventually he or she will lose the ability to adapt. Without warning, the intense fear (the fear is generally irrational) and terror hit you like a Mack truck. You can't breathe, your heart is pounding, you start feeling dizzy, your stomach is lurching, you're feeling cold, and you are convinced you are losing control and going crazy. But guess what? You are not going crazy. Your body is a marvel: As stated before, it is doing exactly what it is supposed to be doing when it perceives danger.

You are now in the *fight or flight* zone. Yes, that is right; you are gearing up to slay the falling crane! Within nanoseconds come the biological changes preparing you for emergency action! The hypothalamus gland sets off a chemical alarm. Your sympathetic nervous system kicks into overdrive,

releasing a flood of stress hormones, adrenalin and noradrenalin from the adrenal glands, and they race through the body,
readying you to run and/or do battle. Major muscle groups
tense in preparation (which explains the aches and pains,
as well as the trembling and shaking). Heart rate and blood
flow to the large muscles increase so you can run faster and
fight harder. Blood vessels constrict to prevent blood loss in
case of injury (which is why you may look pale, and your feet
and hands may feel cold and numb). Pupils dilate so you can
see better (which may cause blurred vision or spots before
your eyes), and your blood sugar ramps up, giving you an
energy boost and speeding up your reaction time. The pace
and depth of your breathing increase, pumping extra oxygen
into the tissues of your muscles (which is why you may experience tightness in the chest or feel as if you are choking,
smothering or cannot catch your breath). Sweat glands jump
to attention, making the skin more slippery and harder for
a predator to grab, while cooling the body to keep it from
overheating.

As all of this takes place, the body processes not essential to immediate survival are suppressed. Your digestive and
reproductive systems slow down (which may produce nausea),
growth hormones are switched off, immune response is shut
down.

Your body is now prepared to do battle.

But what you feel is an overwhelming sense of being trapped
and wanting to escape (signs of that include pacing, foot tap-
ping and snapping at people). The brain immediately narrows
its focus to search your surroundings for danger (making it
difficult to concentrate on daily tasks; over a period of time,
your memory can suffer). You urgently scan the horizon for

your enemy! You are hyperaware and prepared to fight. Bring 'em on! Where are they?! Slowly it dawns on you. There is no monster. There is no falling crane. There is just...you.

Chapter Six

ENEMY NUMBER ONE

"Never interrupt an enemy when he is making a mistake."
—Napoleon Bonaparte

"If there's nothing out there making me anxious, then there must be something wrong with me." That's right. You are Enemy Number One! Down the rabbit hole you go. "I'm going crazy!" "I'm having a heart attack!" "I must be dying!" "I'm losing it!" "I'm out of control!" Sound familiar? The problem is, once you hit this switch, your general anxiety turns into a full-blown panic attack.

"Wait! Wait! Wait! What? Why? How did we get from anxiety to panic?" you ask. "I'm still confused as to why I'm having anxiety!" Why? Because when you tell yourself, "THE CRANE IS FALLING!" you immediately trigger the *fight or flight* response. As the RESEARCHER, you already know what is going to happen: Your healthy body goes to work to protect you, and suddenly all of those physical and emotional sensations kick in. You have just stepped into THE PANIC AND ANXIETY ZONE!

How you perceive the next few seconds will determine how long the attack will last (a few minutes, a few hours, a few days). It is all up to you.

It is very easy to understand the *fight or flight* response when you experience a traumatic event. When the *fight or flight* response hits you out of the clear blue…well, that is confusing. And what is truly difficult to understand is why the *fight or flight* response is already in high gear when you wake up in the morning. What is up with that? It makes no sense! I mean, have you been telling yourself something in your sleep?

Maybe, maybe not. Life is suddenly full of "maybes." Maybe it was just a bad dream. Maybe it was that food you ate last night. Maybe you shouldn't have gone to that party; otherwise, you could have finished your work, and then you wouldn't be feeling this pressure. Maybe you should have taken that pill. FORGET THE DAMN MAYBES! *MAYBE* HAS NOTHING TO DO WITH THIS.

And have you noticed how all those "should haves" and "could haves" have just shown up? What is up with them? Have you not had enough of them, too? Watch out for those energy suckers; they will drain the life right out of you. "Should haves" and "could haves" are nothing more than the pressure of societal expectations. You are already carrying the weight of the world on your shoulders; you do not need the weight of guilt and shame on top of it. What happened to compassion? What happened to being your own loving parent? Get a grip and recite the second most important mantra of this book, the serenity prayer…

> "…grant me the serenity to accept the things I cannot
> change; courage to change the things I can;
> and wisdom to know the difference."
> —*Karl Paul Reinhold Neibuhr*

Read this serenity prayer again, and really understand its meaning. The worrying has to stop! Worry is nothing more

than ruminating about things over which you have no control. Next, you need to erase the WHAT IFS, the SHOULD
HAVES and the COULD HAVES from your vocabulary. They
do nothing but push the falling crane button, which in turn
keeps you in the anxiety and panic mode.

"But how do I do that?" you ask.

By countering all of that negativity with reality. Let's start
with the obvious.

"I'M GOING CRAZY!"

Oh, really? How many times have you told yourself this? And
how many times have you actually gone crazy? How many
times have you run down the street screaming gibberish about
aliens eating your brain and implanting embryos in your
head? I am betting, none. You are not going crazy. Stop telling
yourself that!

"I'M LOSING CONTROL OF MYSELF!"

This is my personal favorite. Boy, can you create great scenarios with this one. Fear of racing around killing people
while yelling obscenities before finally hyperventilating and
passing out. Or better yet, the total opposite. Fear that you will
be frozen, unable to move, almost as if you were paralyzed.

First of all, as you know, neither of these scenarios has
ever happened. Why do you keep telling yourself this kind of
thing? Second, you have already learned that the *fight or flight*
response gears you up to run and escape, not to hurt innocent
people. You are feeling distracted and "out of it" because that
is a mechanism in the *fight or flight* response. The quickest way
to get over the "I am losing control" issue is to remind yourself
that you never had "control" in the first place. Control is an

illusion. Think about it. Over what do you really have control?

"IF THESE ATTACKS KEEP UP,
I'M GOING TO HAVE A NERVOUS BREAKDOWN!"

This one speaks for itself. Scientific evidence has proven that nerves cannot break down. They are with us forever. What is happening to you is in your mind, not in your nerves! Stop being so dramatic! How many times have you had a nervous breakdown?

"I'M HAVING A HEART ATTACK!"

This one is easy. By now, you have seen your general practitioner and, I hope, had an EKG, so you should already know that you DO NOT have heart disease and are in good physical health. However, let us say you suddenly feel breathless, your heart is palpitating, and you have chest pain. Suddenly the voice starts: "Oh, my God, I'm having a heart attack!" No. Sorry. Odds are you are not. Symptoms of a heart attack are usually brought on during exertion. You were just sitting there at your desk, or in your car, or in your bed, worrying about something. Were you not? With panic and anxiety, you can have these symptoms at rest as well as during exertion. This is not the case with heart disease.

The facts are simple. The emotional and physical symptoms of panic and anxiety are uncomfortable, but THEY ARE NOT GOING TO HARM YOU. As the RESEARCHER, you understand what is happening to your body. You also understand that the fleeting moments of "terror" are not terror at all. They are a direct response to the chemicals that have been released into your bloodstream for one purpose and one purpose only: to protect you. They will be freely floating in your system for moments, hours or days, depending on the action you decide to take.

You have two options.

You can continue to be a victim of panic and anxiety, and follow the old destructive pattern. Or, as the RESEARCHER, you can embark on an exciting new journey that will give you the tools to lay this panic and anxiety issue to rest forever.

The choice is yours.

Chapter Seven

STINKING THINKING

"I haven't failed. I've just found 10,000 ways that won't work."
—*Thomas Edison*

If you have ever achieved anything from worrying, please contact me and let me know how you accomplished that. The best place to start your recovery is right here. I want you to keep a journal for one day. Every time a negative thought crosses your mind, I want you to write it in your journal. (If the thought hits you while you are driving, please do us all a favor and pull over to the side of the road before writing it down.) I promise that by the end of the day, you will have a clearer understanding of what is feeding your panic and/or anxiety.

Repetitive negativity does nothing but exhaust you and wear you down! Where is it all coming from? Science has reported that humans have anywhere from fifty thousand to seventy thousand thoughts a day. Up to seventy percent of those thoughts are repetitive. Add panic and anxiety, and BINGO, you are primed and ready to throw yourself the biggest negativity party the world has ever seen.

You have already established that identifying negative thoughts is the most important part of the process here. It's your repetitive thinking that pushes the falling crane button, which, in turn, sends you into the *fight or flight* response, which jump-starts your body's physical and emotional responses.

Now you are primed and ready to go! Panic and anxiety, your two best friends, rush you to your seat, skipping the coming attractions and racing you right to the main event.

Let me stop you here before you start the same old movie. You have a choice. Do you want to watch this horror movie? Or do you want to go next door and watch that great adventure film? The answer is quite simple. Isn't it? So simple, in fact, that you have already gotten out of your seat, hurried over and plopped yourself down to watch the great adventure film.

However, this is not the new behavior you are looking for; deceptively, this is your old behavior. This is the kind of thinking that has gotten you into trouble all along. I call it Stinking Thinking! You will do anything to keep from feeling uncomfortable. This is called *avoidance*, and history has shown that it has not worked for you. So it is just a matter of time until that great adventure film turns into your worst nightmare.

Avoidance will creep insidiously into your life if you let it. For instance, if you suffer an attack while driving on the freeway, your brain makes the incorrect assumption that the freeway was the culprit. Naturally, you start avoiding the freeway. What happens if you have an attack while in the elevator, or in a movie theater, or at the grocery store? You start to avoid those places, too. Before you know it, you have become a prisoner in your own home, afraid to make a move, because you will do anything to keep from having another attack!

But wait!

You are forgetting something! You are the RESEARCHER. You know by now that thoughts and feelings cannot hurt you. They are just thoughts and feelings.

As a matter of fact, when panic and anxiety appear, you

learn pretty quickly that, as in a classic horror movie, things are not what they appear to be. Take *Frankenstein,* for example, a masterpiece of literature. Dr. Frankenstein creates a "monster," who really wants nothing more than love and acceptance. His creator, his "father," is the true monster for rejecting and abandoning his son.

Every time you run from your panic and anxiety, you are doing the exact same thing, telling yourself that you are not lovable or acceptable. It is time to face the monster head on. Look him straight in the eye and say, "I know you, I recognize you, and I am going to learn to love you."

The physiological responses to panic and anxiety should no longer be a mystery. If they are, you need to go back and reread the beginning of this book.

Knowledge is power.

The better you understand your body's physical and emotional responses, the faster you will be able to get rid of the fear associated with them. No, you are not dying. No, you are not going crazy. And no, with a purported hundreds of millions of people worldwide suffering from panic and anxiety, you are definitely not alone.

Yes, the attacks are horribly uncomfortable, but they are not life threatening. The chemicals and hormones will run their course, and you will soon learn to relax through the process.

"Learn to relax? What, are you crazy? How is that possible?"

After keeping your one day's journal, you should have discovered that negativity runs your life, that at least seventy percent of your thoughts are negative. Odds are very good that before your last panic or anxiety attack, you were telling yourself something pretty horrific, which started the cycle.

With your journal, you now have a great tool. As the

RESEARCHER, you can track the thoughts and events leading to your panic and anxiety attacks, as well as the thoughts and events that follow. Your triggers will become apparent, and that understanding will give you the tools to work on them, even become friends with them.

Unraveling this information is a process. How quickly that happens will be determined by your willingness to do the homework. Eventually you will no longer have to run from your triggers. You will develop a more clinical approach, and you will get to know each and every one of them intimately. Once you do that, you will no longer fear them.

Imagine what you can do if you take your negative repetitive thoughts and turn them into positive ones. By deciphering your triggers, that is exactly what you will accomplish. You will not only reclaim the life you thought you had, you will start to create the life you have always dreamed of.

Now start writing!

Chapter Eight

STOP WORRYING YOURSELF SICK

"Today is the tomorrow we worried about yesterday."
—*Author unknown*

Take a good look at the notes you have made in your journal. Without knowing it, you have been worrying yourself sick; it is pretty obvious, isn't it? There are distinct differences between worry and concern. *Worry* is ruminating about things over which you have no control, while *concern* is action based. I have no doubt that when you examine your notes, you will discover that ninety-nine percent of them relate to things over which you have absolutely no control. If you were taking action, you would not be sitting there worrying.

Here are a few examples.

"I'M WORRIED I'M GOING TO LOSE MY JOB!"
Okay.

Why are you worried? Are you doing your job? Are you getting to work on time? Are you performing what is expected of you? Are you a team player? If your answers to these questions are yes, then what are you worrying about?

If your answers to these questions are no, then these are concerns you can do something about. You can take action to make sure you do not lose your job: You can get to work on time; you can perform the work that is expected of you; you can learn to be a team player.

However, if you are sitting there worrying whether the company is going to downsize, go bankrupt or relocate, these are matters over which you have no control, so why are you giving them any energy?

"NO ONE WILL EVER LIKE ME! I'M ALL ALONE!"

Would you call these worries or concerns?

These statements are driven by nothing but WORRY and FEAR. You have absolutely no control over someone liking you or leaving you, or what may occur in the future. And hundreds of millions of people experience panic and anxiety, so you are definitely not on this journey all alone! Are you?

"WHO'S GOING TO WANT ME?"

Right now, with that negative outlook, no one! Be honest. Even you are tired of you right now. Yet if you take action and turn the negative into a positive, everyone will want to be around you.

"THEY'RE ALL GOING TO LEAVE ME!"

You bet they are. People do not want to be around negativity. It's pretty safe to say that, by now, you have exhausted everyone around you. But if you take action, and turn the negative into a positive, there's a good chance no one is going to leave anyone. Just remember, control is an illusion. Ultimately, you have no control over what other people will do.

"WHAT WILL HAPPEN TO ME?"

This one is easy. If you do nothing, you will be haunted by

panic, fear and anxiety. However, if you take action, PEACE AND SERENITY AWAIT YOU! It's your choice.

"I AM GOING CRAZY!"

Really? If you examine this thought all on its own, it is clearly designed to do nothing but provoke panic and anxiety. First of all, truly crazy people have severe psychiatric disorders. If you had one, you probably would have been diagnosed by now; of that, you can be sure. You are not going crazy! You feel as if you are going crazy because you perceive that you have no control over these feelings and symptoms.

Now is the time for me to give you the most important mantra of this book:

"This feels uncomfortable, but since I've experienced these feelings and thoughts before, I know they are transitory. I know they are going to pass."

This mantra should be applied to every negative thought that comes into your head. As soon as "I am going crazy" enters your mind, counter it immediately with a positive thought, follow it with the mantra, and repeat the positive thought once more.

For example: "I'M GOING CRAZY!"

Stop a moment and take a slow, deep breath. When you exhale, counter the refrain "I'm going crazy" with a positive thought: **"I'm healthy!"** Then say your mantra: **"This feels uncomfortable, but since I've experienced these feelings and thoughts before, I know they are transitory. I know they are going to pass."**

And then repeat your positive thought. "I AM HEALTHY!"

It is important to cancel the negative thought and replace

it immediately with a positive one.

"But—" you say.

No! No "buts"!

It truly is that simple. Cancel the negative thought with a positive thought.

Watch how to apply this practice to the next statement.

"I'M GOING TO BE ALL ALONE!"

No denying it; this is a big one for all of us. And you continue to undermine yourself with this fear. You already know that hundreds of millions of people around the world are suffering from panic and/or anxiety. That means YOU ARE NOT ALONE! In fact, the odds are very good that many people in your circle of life are experiencing the same feelings you are. They just may be afraid to talk about them. When the thought **"I'm all alone!"** raises its ugly head, look it square in the eye, take a deep breath, exhale, and counter it with a positive thought: **"Millions of people are experiencing these same feelings and thoughts right now. I'm not alone!"**

Immediately follow up with your mantra: **"This feels uncomfortable, but since I've experienced these feelings and thoughts before, I know they are transitory. I know they are going to pass."**

Then repeat the positive statement: **"Millions of people are experiencing these same feelings and thoughts right now. I'm not alone!"**

If you have to repeat this pattern a hundred times to shut up that negative voice, so be it.

You can apply this principle to every negative thought you have written in your journal. Start today; start now. Leave the past behind. Do not care about what happened yesterday, last week, last month, last year or ten years ago. Do not care about what will happen tomorrow, next week, next month, next year or ten years from now. All you want to care about is what is happening RIGHT NOW!

If you follow this simple process—countering the negative thought with a positive thought and repeating your mantra— you will no longer be a prisoner of panic and anxiety. You will start living the life you were born to live.

Please remember, this is a gentle exercise. This is about LOVE and HOPE. This is about learning how to love YOU all over again. It is as if you are retraining yourself on a cellular level.

Love conquers all fear. A great example is the story of a dog I rescued. She had been severely abused. She was a year old and had never been allowed out of her cage for more than a few minutes at a time. No attention or love had ever been given her. From her smell, it was obvious she had never been washed, and from the looks of her, she had barely been fed. She was filled with such panic and anxiety, she did nothing but shake with fear.

When she was brought to me, my initial desire was to take her out of the cage and throw the cage away. But after watching her for a few minutes, I realized that to her, the cage was home. My job was to give her as much love and attention as I possibly could, until she realized the cage was no longer her destiny.

I removed her from the filthy cage and then scrubbed and cleaned it, putting a soft, comfortable towel in it for her to sleep on. My next task was to give her a bath. Her little body was tight and tense, but when she felt the warm water, she started to relax. Her reaction was amazing; I could feel her energy changing. And yet, by the time I had her dry, she was tense again, so I put her back in her open cage.

For the next few days, I gave her all the love and attention I could, and in less than a week, she was playing with toys and sleeping in my bed with me. In another few months, you would not have recognized that dog. When I was home, she demanded to be in my lap. She was happy, loving, playful, protective…everything she was born to be.

Love conquers fear.

This book is about self-love. It is about learning to be loving, patient and understanding to YOU, not just to your friends, family and animals. With lots of self-love, you will be able to accomplish anything you set your heart and mind to.

Chapter Nine

BREATHING FOR YOUR LIFE

"If you woke up breathing, congratulations!
You have another chance."
—*Andrea Boydston*

One of the most overlooked, cost effective, time efficient and powerful tools in combating panic and anxiety is...breathing. If you feel panic and/or anxiety, you most likely are doing one of two things: holding your breath or hyperventilating.

True, when we are born, we gasp our first breath. But loving Mother Nature steps in, takes over and calmly institutes abdominal-thoracic breath support. It is our natural breathing state; once asleep, we revert to it.

Yet somehow along the way, you have probably lost the art of breathing using your abdominal muscles. There are many possible reasons: poor posture, holding your abdomen in so you can have the perfect abs, wearing too-tight clothing, asthma, stress, panic, anxiety. The culprit does not matter. You only need to care that your breathing is not centered in your upper chest but in your abdomen, where Mother Nature intended it to be. That's why it is called the Abdominal-Thoracic Breath-Support System.

Breathing centered in your abdomen keeps your body in

the parasympathetic state. This means that your heart rate stays low, your breathing is slow and natural, your blood pressure is normal, your muscles are relaxed, and you feel a sense of calm and ease.

The body needs a certain amount of oxygen and carbon dioxide to work cohesively. But if you are over-breathing through your upper chest—otherwise known as hyperventilating—you are throwing yourself out of the parasympathetic state and into the *fight or flight* response. Then come the symptoms of panic and/or anxiety: rapid heartbeat, racing thoughts, dizziness, numbness in the hands or feet, shortness of breath, nausea, etc. As we have learned, when these reactions kick in, your body is telling your mind, "The crane is falling!"

The quickest way to stop the *fight or flight* response is through relaxation. Remember, it is a physical impossibility to experience panic or anxiety if you are relaxed. By shifting your focus to proper breathing, you can reverse the symptoms and return the body to its natural, organic state of calmness.

How do you accomplish this? Simply by breathing.

It is a sad reality that in our society, people learn how to drive but not how to breathe. Let's get to work.

Proper breathing is an art unto itself. You have heard many names for this kind of breathing: belly breathing, abdominal breathing, diaphragmatic breathing. *Diaphragmatic breathing*, however, is inaccurate and will focus your breathing incorrectly. You do not want to breathe from your upper chest. By now, you know that if you are feeling fearful, you tend to hold your breath or take many shallow breaths. It is extremely important to distinguish the difference between *breathing supported by your abdomen/belly*, which *fills the lungs*, and breathing from your upper chest, which does not.

Let's establish the proper breathing technique. Sit in a comfortable chair, feet flat on the ground. Place one hand on your chest and the other on your belly/abdomen. Breathe in and out for a few minutes without altering your normal breathing pattern. Which hand is moving? The hand on the chest? Or the hand on the belly/abdomen? It's quite likely that the chest hand is bobbing up and down, which means you are breathing from your upper chest. In order to break this bad habit, you are going to retrain yourself.

When doing these exercises, remember first and foremost that all INHALATIONS are through the NOSE, and all EXHALATIONS are through the MOUTH. Take a few breaths and practice this. Remember to breathe naturally. You do not want to hyperventilate; that is what got you here in the first place.

Once you have mastered proper inhalation and exhalation, cross your arms and put both hands on your upper chest. Now take a breath through your nose, but do not let your upper chest fill first. As your lungs fill completely with air, the sensation should be that your abdomen/belly is filling first, and the upper chest cavity is filling last. This part of the exercise is vital, since it forces you to focus on breathing using your abdomen. Now exhale through your mouth, and repeat.

Practice until you feel confident enough to put your arms down. This new way of breathing will seem a bit strange at first, but soon you will feel the results.

Now we can start the main exercise. The **Four-Seven-Eight Breathing Exercise** is taught by most of the world's top panic and anxiety specialists. Doctors, health practitioners, chiropractors and yoga instructors swear by it. I can honestly tell you that learning how to breathe properly helped save my life.

Please remember to be kind to yourself during this exercise. Do not sit in your chair and judge whether you are doing this correctly. At first, this exercise will seem complicated, but within minutes, you will understand its simplicity. If, at any point, you find you have reverted to the old, improper way of breathing, make the correction and start again.

It's time to get to work.

Many experts suggest this exercise be done while sitting; however, it can also be practiced while lying down or standing up. To prepare:

1. Sit in your chair with your back straight and your hands resting comfortably on your thighs.
2. Look straight ahead and relax your arms and shoulders; this will balance your head and neck. Try not to fix your gaze on anything in particular; partially closing your eyes can help, but if necessary, you can shut them.
3. For a few moments, focus on your breathing. All inhalations should be through your nose; all exhalations, through your mouth.
4. Put the tip of your tongue gently in contact with the top of your mouth, just behind your teeth. Keep the tongue in place throughout the exercise.

The exercise itself:

1. Inhale a nice smooth breath through your nose to a mental count of four seconds. Your lower abdomen and belly should push out and give the sensation of filling with air.
2. Hold your breath for a mental count of seven seconds.
3. Slowly and smoothly, exhale to a mental count of eight seconds. Remember to keep your relaxed tongue in contact with the roof of your mouth.

4. As you exhale, relax your body and focus on letting go of
    your tension and stress.

    You have now completed the first breath.

Pause briefly without inhaling, and then go right into the
next breath, following these instructions until you have finished ten breaths.

You may feel as if you are not getting enough oxygen at
first, but do not worry; with practice, this slower pace will feel
more natural and comfortable.

This breathing exercise should be used at least once a day.
If you are experiencing panic and/or anxiety, it should be used
three times a day.

It's in the nature of the beast to wait until you are feeling
panic and/or anxiety before using this tool. Do not wait. I did
myself a disservice when I first started the Four-Seven-Eight
Breathing Exercise. As I felt better, I stopped doing the exercise. I mean, why not? I was feeling better; I was busy. And it
wasn't as if I didn't breathe all day long, every day of the year.

Then, as soon as a panic or anxiety attack hit, I would
implement the exercise. It was a vicious cycle: I would start
feeling better, and gradually I did the exercise less and less,
until I was not doing it at all. Then the next attack would hit,
and I would start the process all over again. I finally realized
that pattern was getting me nowhere. Why was I sabotaging
myself?

Once I started doing the breathing exercise on a daily
basis, I discovered that not only was I feeling better, I had
more energy. Without knowing it, I had created a solid tool
against stress. Whenever I felt stressed—at home, work, even
on vacation—I could use this tool with immediate calming

effects. Who would have thought a simple breathing exercise could create such a change in my life? But that is exactly what happened.

The great thing about this exercise is that it can be done anywhere. I use it at home, at work, on a plane, in bed, on the beach…you name it. Since there is a tendency to close your eyes, however, do not operate any sort of machinery or vehicle while practicing this technique!

Because you can do this simple exercise anywhere, there is no reason not to do it at least once a day. It is an effective tool if used properly; like anything else, you will get out of it what you put into it.

Remember, it takes many links in the chain to create panic and/or anxiety. By removing one link, you are well on your way to successfully stopping your panic and anxiety.

What are you waiting for? Start breathing for your life!

Chapter Ten

RUNNING ON EMPTY

"One cannot think well, love well, or sleep well,
if one has not dined well."
—*Virginia Woolf*

W hen it comes to panic and/or anxiety, it is important to view your body as what it is: the most amazing, technologically advanced, high-performance racing machine on the planet. Before you took your first breath, this marvel was already hard at work creating the systems running your engine today. However, in order for your engine to function properly, you have to give it the proper fuel and additives.

We have all heard the old adage: *You are what you eat.* With panic and/or anxiety, we are going to modify the adage: *You are what you eat and drink*! Do not forget, over half of the human body is made up of water.

Science has proven that what you eat and drink affects your physical and mental performance. By choosing foods wisely, you will not only build a stronger physical body but, more important, you will put into place building blocks to strengthen your emotional mental health. If your tank is empty, you are going to feel run down and anxious. If your tank is full, your engine has the opportunity to achieve optimum performance. Why just an opportunity? Because it will do you no good to fill your gasoline engine with diesel fuel.

There is no doubt that food is one of the great pleasures of the world. You do need to remember that while it tastes good now, it might not make you feel good later. How do those two statements correlate? In order to explain it properly, I need to provide a quick biology lesson.

Neurotransmitters are chemicals that relay, amplify and modulate signals between a neuron and another cell, transmitting thoughts and actions to the brain. The only thing a neurotransmitter does directly is to activate one or more types of receptors on the end of the neurons, which dictate the neurotransmitter's effect. Certain foods help boost the receptors, making the neurons very happy, and thus making us feel happy (an important concept to remember when we get to the supplement and medication chapters).

Imagine a chandelier. This *chandelier* represents our *brain*. Each of the arms of the chandelier holds a light bulb; the *light bulbs* represent the *neurons*. For these light bulbs to work, there must be a filament inside to receive the signal; the *filament* represents the *receptor*. In order to light the bulb, the receptor needs electricity; the *electricity* is our *neurotransmitter*.

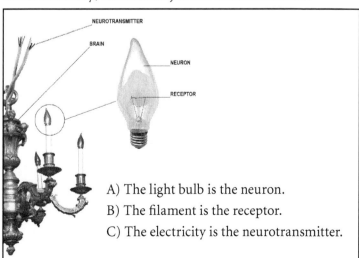

NEUROTRANSMITTER

BRAIN

NEURON

RECEPTOR

A) The light bulb is the neuron.
B) The filament is the receptor.
C) The electricity is the neurotransmitter.

Neurotransmitters are chemical messengers, and these messengers are created from the food you eat. With panic and/ or anxiety, the two most important neurotransmitters are serotonin and dopamine, otherwise known as the "feel good" neurotransmitters.

SEROTONIN is the *Zen Buddhist neurotransmitter*: It regulates mood, tranquility, sleep, temperature, memory, emotions, etc.

DOPAMINE is the *Risk Taker neurotransmitter,* providing pleasure, power, enthusiasm, motivation. It plays a significant role in the Reward System (chemicals that spread out into a network and create what is known as a "cascade" affect that leaves one feeling secure, calm, comfortable and satisfied). Dopamine is associated with arousal, love and addiction.

What does all this mean? It means that, with careful consideration given to the foods you put into your body, you have the ability to affect both of these "feel good" neurotransmitters, thus allowing you to unlock yet another link in the chain of panic and anxiety.

Before discussing the super foods that will help boost your body, mind and mood, I need to explain the difference between proteins and carbohydrates.

PROTEINS (foods like cheese, eggs, fish, legumes, meat, poultry, tofu) boost your energy and alertness. COMPLEX CARBOHYDRATES (fruits, pasta, vegetables, whole grains) are your relaxing and calming foods. Notice the word *complex*? All carbohydrates break down into glucose, which the body uses as fuel. Simple carbohydrates (sugar, sucrose, fructose, corn syrup, white or wheat flour) are digested quickly. Complex carbohydrates take longer for the body to metabolize and digest, so the body and brain have time to absorb and use the fuel (glucose) they provide before the excess is stored as fat. Because simple carbohydrates take less time to digest, they flood the body with excess amounts of fuel. Our cells rarely require large amounts of energy at one time, so it is likely the glucose (sugar) is going to be converted to fat. Simple or complex, in too large a quantity, carbohydrates can make you feel lethargic and sleepy.

With a little understanding as to how your body and brain utilize carbohydrates and proteins, you can start using them as tools to help you feel better. Carbohydrates help raise the levels of serotonin, while protein increases the levels of dopamine. These, as I mentioned before, are your "feel good" neurotransmitters. Low levels of either carbohydrates or protein are going to make you feel anxious.

That is why this chapter is not about dieting.

Have you ever been around someone on a diet? After a couple of weeks, he or she is ready to kill everyone in sight. Why? Because most diets have you cut out carbohydrates. And what happens? Your blood-sugar levels drop too low to sustain the optimal levels of serotonin in your brain. Low levels of serotonin can cause anxiety, depression, insomnia, panic attacks, PMS, obesity, bulimia.

These yo-yo diets can affect your dopamine levels as well. Low levels of dopamine can create bad moods and depression, poor memory, low libido, inability to concentrate, weight gain, cravings, addictions, fatigue.

Starting today, you have two goals: to learn which carbohydrates, proteins and fats are best at boosting your mood neurotransmitters; and to learn what time of day to eat these carbohydrates, proteins and fats to get the maximum results from your neurotransmitters, creating optimum mental health.

Before we discuss these two goals, here is a list of things you should avoid:

ALCOHOL

As alcohol is metabolized in the body, serotonin (Zen Master) neurotransmitter levels temporarily increase, so you feel calm for a while. The dopamine (Risk Taker) neurotransmitter levels also increase temporarily, which is why your inhibitions and boundaries start to relax. At first, it all feels good, but then, as the alcohol starts to wear off, the "feel good" neurotransmitters are depleted. Hangovers, insomnia and our old friends panic and anxiety show up, and before you know it, you need to increase the amount of alcohol you drink to keep up with the ups and downs. It is a no-win situation. Because it is readily available and socially acceptable, alcohol is the number one drug of choice for people struggling with panic and anxiety. It does not take a genius to figure out that if you are taking any supplements or medications for panic and/or anxiety, you should not be drinking alcohol!

The solution: Drink water.

CAFFEINE

Caffeine works by stimulating the central nervous system. It arouses the body. Mimicking panic and anxiety symptoms, it can make you feel nervous, restless and jittery, which means your brain is going to tell you that you are feeling panic and anxiety. Need I say more? Quit.

The solution: Drink water.

The body is at least sixty percent water. Alcohol and caffeine work as diuretics, increasing fluid output, which can lead to dehydration. Dehydration, however slight, can cause anxiety. It is important to stay hydrated. If you wait until you are thirsty to drink, you are already dehydrated. Doctors recommend you drink at least eight glasses of liquid (water, fruit juices, milk, soup, sports drinks, etc.) a day. That should be adjusted (more, not less) with heat and exercise.

NICOTINE

Nicotine is the big bad wolf of all stimulants. Seven seconds after being inhaled, nicotine increases the levels of dopamine (you know, the Risk Taker neurotransmitter) in your body, releasing adrenaline into the bloodstream and triggering your *fight or flight* response. A few minutes after you finish a cigarette, the nicotine levels in your blood drop. With nicotine withdrawal, your mood drops. Agitation, inability to concentrate, insomnia and fatigue set in, and suddenly it is time to light up again.

The solution: Quit! This drug is directly affecting your panic and/or anxiety!

Please remember that alcohol, caffeine and nicotine

are extremely addicting. As with any drug, it is best to taper off slowly, which may require medical supervision.

ARTIFICIAL PRESERVATIVES, ADDITIVES, MSG,
ASPERTAME, ETC.

Reactions to these substances vary from mild to extreme. They have been proven to cause vitamin B1 deficiencies, which directly affects emotional stability.

The solution: Eat as much fresh food as possible. None of us is perfect. By cutting out ninety percent of the processed foods in your daily diet, you will be well on your way to a healthier mind and body.

SUGAR

This simple carbohydrate dives right into the bloodstream and revs up the engine, pumping insulin into your system, sending you to the moon and back. Unfortunately, that means your blood-sugar levels have gone up and down, kicking in your adrenal hormones, which means you are now on the sugar blues express.

The solution: I know, I know; it is almost impossible to avoid sugar. Cut back as much as you can. When you do consume it, make sure you eat it with other foods, because this will help slow the entry of sugar into your bloodstream. In other words, SUGAR SHOULD BE YOUR DESSERT, NOT YOUR MEAL!

It does not take an expert to understand this basic information. With panic and/or anxiety, all you have to do is pay attention to the way your body responds to the things you eat and drink. The following foods will help give your body, mind and soul what it needs to keep you healthy, happy and calm.

CARBOHYDRATES

Fruit: apples, apricots, avocado, berries, cherries, grapes, grapefruit, oranges, pineapple, pears, plums, tangerines, watermelon, etc.

Legumes: adzuki beans, anasazi beans, black beans, black-eyed peas, chickpeas, edamame, fava beans, lentils, lima beans, pinto beans, red kidney beans

Pasta: whole-grain pastas

Root vegetables: artichokes, beets, carrots, potatoes, radishes, sweet potatoes, yams, etc.

Vegetables: bell peppers, broccoli, cabbage, corn, garlic, mushrooms, onions, spinach, tomatoes

Whole-grain foods: brown rice, oats, rice bran, whole wheat, barley, etc.

PROTEINS
Dairy products: cheese, cottage cheese, skim milk, yogurt
Eggs: omega-3 eggs
Fish: salmon, halibut, snapper, tuna, sardines, mackerel
Meat: beef, lamb, pork
Poultry: turkey, chicken
Seafood: lobster, shrimp, scallops
Soy: tofu, soymilk, edamame

How many of these foods are you consuming on a regular basis? Are they fresh? Or are they pre-packaged, frozen, stick-it-in-a-microwave-for-three-minutes, grab-a-diet-cola and-sit-in-front-of-the-television foods?

You know what happens when you put cheap gas in your car. The engine knocks, pings, and rattles and rolls. Why would you think your body is any different? Starting today, starting right now, you need to look at your body as the performance machine it is, and treat it accordingly.

So far, I've discussed only the body's fuels. It is time to take a look at the lubricants. About two-thirds of the brain is made up of fats. Fats play a crucial role in regulating mood, memory, circulation, inflammation and your immune system. That is why people on low-fat diets have a higher risk of panic and/ or anxiety. However, all fats are not created equal. Our brains require specific fats, so put down that butter!

Two fats are extremely important to our mental health: omega-3 and omega-9 (monosaturated oleic acid, one of the most common fatty acids found in the brain).

The following is a list of brain- and heart-friendly fats.

FATS, NUTS, FRUITS and SEEDS
Butters: almond, cashew, macadamia, peanut, pecan, walnut
Oils: almond, canola, macadamia, olive, peanut, pecan
Nuts: almonds, cashews, walnuts, peanuts, pecans, macadamia and Brazil nuts
Fruits: açaí, avocado
Seeds: sesame, pumpkin, flax

The goal is to incorporate these foods and fats into your daily diet. It is best to eat frequent small meals. We all know what happens when you skip a meal. At first, you feel as if you are experiencing an energy high, then your blood-sugar levels drop, and you start feeling irritable and nervous; you might even get the shakes. If you go too long without eating, you can pass out. These physical reactions mimic your experience of panic and/or anxiety, and your brain cannot differentiate between them. Before you know it, panic and anxiety are front and center, and you are frantically scanning the horizon as your brain screams, "The crane is falling!"

Fortunately, you now have the proper tools to keep that from happening. You have learned that: a) complex carbohydrates can increase serotonin levels; b) proteins can increase dopamine levels; c) fats are necessary for the body and brain to function; and d) water is your body's key element.

The final step in the equation is learning *when* to eat the carbohydrates, proteins and fats, so you get the maximum results from your neurotransmitters.

The single most important meal of the day is breakfast. *Breakfast* means just that: breaking the fast that you have been on since you ate the night before. Skipping this meal means you are depleting your stored "feel good" neurotransmitters, which will leave you feeling irritable, tired and anxious and diminish your ability to focus.

Your goal is to fill your body, that miraculous engine, with the best fuel available as often as possible.

You want energy and peak mental performance during the day. To that end, breakfast and lunch should be low in calories, high in protein and moderate in the amount of sugars containing complex carbohydrates. If you want to relax in the evening, dinner should be high in calories, carbohydrates and tryptophan-containing proteins. As we have already discussed, carbohydrates help stimulate the "feel good" neurotransmitter serotonin. That is why dinnertime is the best time to have that small dessert you have been craving all day.

As the RESEARCHER, after absorbing all this information, you now know why it is essential that your breakfast be nutritious and balanced, consisting of equal amounts of complex carbohydrates and proteins. These two energy sources create synergy: Grains + Dairy/Soy + Fruit provide everything your body needs to start your day the right way.

Examples of a balanced breakfast are:

Whole-grain bagel, low-fat cream cheese/Tofuti and salmon, with a piece of fruit; scrambled eggs, whole-grain toast, milk or orange juice; oatmeal, fresh berries and yogurt.

It is important not to overeat. In fact, *you should feel hungry between meals.* Have a piece of fruit, a protein bar or some trail mix, or roll up a slice of meat with cheese and eat a few crackers. If you eat right, your energy level will stay consistent throughout the day, which means your mood will stay consistent as well.

Your body is a remarkable machine and deserves to be treated with respect. Eat as many raw, natural, organic, pesticide-free foods as you can find. When you select your meat and poultry proteins, make the hormone-free choice if you can.

What are you waiting for? Open your refrigerator and your pantry, and with the new tools and information you have been given, make the choices that are going to soothe your mind, body and mood.

Chapter Eleven

TRICKS AND TREATS

"The quickest way to achieve relaxation…is by taking action!"
—Judson Rothschild

Today, right here, right now, you will discover a tool you can apply in your daily life that forever will alter the course of how you feel. This chapter is about *action*. It is about making choices that will not only make you feel better but will make you look better. Let's face the facts: Things have not been looking so good lately, have they? That is all going to change, right now!

I have already addressed three links in the panic and anxiety chain: negative self-talk, breathing and nutrition. The following tricks and treats are designed to break that chain. That is, if you want that to happen badly enough. Frankly, you will get out of this exactly what you put into it. You will need to make a one hundred percent commitment, because fifty percent just will not do it. And you know that, because you are still reading this book.

As you have already learned, medical science clearly has proven **it is a physical impossibility to experience panic and/ or anxiety if the body and mind are in a relaxed state.** So the goal here is simple: to apply every tool you can, on a daily basis, to bring about a state of relaxation. The following tools are designed to do just that!

EXERCISE

Science has shown us that exercise is a vital tool in breaking the panic and anxiety chain. How does it work? Very simply. Exercise increases blood flow to the brain, thus increasing mood-enhancing neurotransmitters, boosting the feel-good endorphins that will have a positive effect on your mood while diminishing muscle tension and stress. Exercise builds self-confidence, creates a distraction, allows for social interaction, reduces overall fatigue, enhances overall cognitive function, and improves thinking and mental function—which also improves the ability to sleep!

The science is rock solid regarding exercise and its effect on depression, panic and anxiety. Many therapists who specialize in these areas refuse to take on patients who will not make the commitment to exercise three to five days a week.

What does that tell you?

It tells you that exercise is a win-win; it will do nothing but make you feel better. Trust me, no one starts out loving or liking exercise. When you are in the throes of panic and/or anxiety, it is hard to think of doing anything, let alone finding the motivation to get out of the house. However, you cannot wait for motivation to find you; you have to find it. The only way to do that is by taking action. You have to get up, get out and do something!

Thirty minutes of exercise five days a week has been proven to be one of the best non-pharmacological antidepressants in the world. The best way to start this program is to identify what type of exercise and activities you enjoy. If none comes to mind, then you need to open the front door and start walking very fast until you come up with a list of things you enjoy doing that will get your heart racing. You do not have time to sit around and think about this. You need to get your body moving right now.

At the same time, it is important to realize that during exercise, your physiological responses change. Your heart rate increases, your body perspires, and you feel as if you are out of breath. All of these are normal functions of the body that mimic the panic and anxiety experience. You are not having a heart, panic or anxiety attack; these are just normal physiological responses to exercise. Remember that, and do not push the "crane is falling!" button.

The goal, and the key to exercise, is this: Make it a game and a challenge. You always want to throw something different into the mix. For example, I find nothing more boring than running on a treadmill for thirty minutes. So if I am going to the gym every day for aerobic exercise, I start by getting on the recumbent bike for ten minutes, switch to the treadmill for ten minutes, and do the last ten minutes on the elliptical machine. The following day, I reverse the order, so my body never gets used to this routine. The third day I leave out the treadmill and add the rowing machine. Whatever works to keep you interested in working out is what you need to do.

The great secret to exercise has always been not to get into a routine. One day I will work out at the gym; the next, I will go hiking. The third day I will swim; the fourth, play tennis. The fifth day I will head back to the gym. The following week, I will mix it all up again.

Change is good. The goal here is to have fun while breaking a sweat. What works for me may not work for you, which is why you need to make a list of the things that you enjoy doing. Better yet, add things that you have always wanted to do, and gradually integrate them into your life, five days a week.

After you establish that list, the next step is to determine the best time of day for you to work out and achieve your goals. Some of us are more motivated in the afternoon than in the morning, and vice versa. Work schedules play an important part in this. It does not make any difference if you work out in the morning or in the afternoon; you just need to make sure you work out.

That is the game plan, pure and simple.

You do want to avoid working out after 7:30 in the evening, because your body needs a certain amount of time for the endorphins to quiet down so you can fall sleep. (More on sleep in the next chapter.)

Getting to the gym is a priority. It gets you out of your house or apartment, you can socialize, and, more important, you can see other people getting into shape. There is no better motivator than seeing other people work out! If you have been feeling shame about the way your body looks and feels, look around you: You are not alone. That is why it is important to get out of the house and work out. If you need more motivation, work out with a friend or hire a trainer.

Some of you are probably thinking, "This guy is crazy! He doesn't get it. I am so depressed and anxiety ridden, I hardly have the motivation to get out of bed, let alone go work out!" Believe me, I do get it. I remember thinking those exact same thoughts...for months! Where is my drive? My desire? Why don't I have any energy? Why can't I do this? I felt like a total failure.

I had anticipatory anxiety just thinking about exercising, fearing it would somehow bring on more panic and anxiety. Finally, sick of feeling frustrated and anxious, I picked up the phone and sent SOS's out to my family and friends. One of my best friends came over, and we went walking. Being athletic, I had never looked at walking as exercise. But after thirty minutes of walking and talking, I realized I was out of breath and sweating. More important, I was up and out of the house! We made plans to walk three times that week. I started interspersing those walks with workouts at the gym, and after a few weeks, I started feeling much better.

The point of this story is simple: If you are not an athlete and have never enjoyed sports and/or cannot afford the gym, start walking, because walking is great exercise. No more excuses. Get up, open the door, walk down the street for fifteen minutes, then walk back. Before you know it, thirty minutes has passed, and you have accomplished your daily goal. So get going. No more excuses!

Pay attention to your body, though, and do not do too much in the beginning, sabotaging yourself right out of the gate. If you have not been working out, start slowly. The ultimate goal is to do thirty to sixty minutes of exercise a day, five days a week. It does not matter how long it takes you to reach that goal; what matters is that you start working toward it!

Aerobic exercise has been proven to lead to anti-panic and anti-anxiety results, which clearly helps break the cycle of worry and reduces stress. So what are you waiting for? Get started!

YOGA

Yoga is a physical and mental discipline originating in India. For centuries, it has proven to be one of the best relaxation and stress-management tools in the world. There are many styles and forms of yoga, but we are going to focus on Hatha Yoga.

Hatha is the combination of two Sanskrit words: *ha*, meaning sun, and *tha*, meaning moon; when the terms are combined, they mean *forceful*. Hatha Yoga is designed to create greater flexibility while encouraging a calmer mind, using two basic components: controlled breathing and physical poses. Although you can pick up a book or CD describing this type of yoga, with diagrams of the poses, I strongly recommend taking a beginning class. It is important to build a firm foundation while learning yoga, and there is no better way to do that than by having a qualified instructor guide you through the poses.

Some of you may be thinking, Yoga? BORING! But that is far from the case. Yoga has been proven to help alleviate symptoms of depression, panic and anxiety. That is not boring.

Boring is sitting on the sofa feeling sorry for yourself.

Yoga is a workout for the body and the mind. Performed properly, it has numerous physical and emotional benefits.

When you look at the physical benefits, you cannot help but wonder why more people are not doing yoga. While working through the poses, you increase your flexibility, which improves your posture and your range of motion. You gain strength, eye-hand coordination, dexterity, depth perception and balance. Your pulse, blood pressure and respiratory rates decrease, which helps stabilize the autonomic nervous system, a huge bonus for anyone with panic and/or anxiety! Your respiratory and cardiovascular efficiency increase, too, giving you much more energy, increasing your resiliency—and thus your immunity—while helping you to sleep better. The list is almost endless.

As for the emotional benefits…. We have devoted way too much time to avoiding the symptoms of panic and/or anxiety.

Anything that arouses our nervous system, we run from or avoid. Yoga strengthens the nervous system, which in turn calms the feelings of panic and/or anxiety. The breathing and the poses give us something other than ourselves on which to focus. Hatha Yoga improves our attention, memory and concentration, while teaching us self-acceptance and how to manage our involuntary physical reactions.

As we learned in a previous chapter, the ultimate in regard to controlling and balancing the nervous system is the art of breathing. Once you learn this, you will never again hear yourself say, "Oh, no. I am losing control!"

Just as with exercise, it is important to start slowly. A good instructor will encourage you to go at your own speed and will honor your limitations. Just because the person next to you can touch her toes and do the splits does not mean that you have to do so. Yoga is not a competition.

And yoga is not expensive; you do not need special clothes. All you have to do is show up. It is a wonderful way to cultivate and encourage peacefulness through breathing, physical posturing and meditation.

MEDITATION

Meditation takes moments to accomplish, can be performed anywhere and, for the most part, is absolutely free. How can you beat that?

The concept behind meditation is very simple: A relaxed mind equals a relaxed body. In order to relax the mind, you need to keep it out of the past and the future, and learn to BE in the present moment.

Sounds easy, right? Wrong.

If you were already good at doing that, you would not be

feeling panic and/or anxiety. Meditation is one of the most important tools in your arsenal against those feelings. It can produce a deep state of relaxation as you learn how to let go of the endless chatter, information and tasks pulsing through your brain.

Benefits of meditation:

Relaxation

Increased sense of well-being

Inner peace

Increased energy

Improved concentration

Lower oxygen consumption

Decreased respiratory rate

These are the same benefits that exercise and yoga produce.

There are two basic types of meditation: concentrative meditation and mindfulness meditation. *Concentrative meditation* requires you to focus on your breathing plus an image or a sound (a word or mantra). *Mindfulness meditation* requires you to focus on the present moment, encouraging you to be aware of your thoughts while maintaining detachment. The latter can be very difficult to achieve while dealing with panic and anxiety, so let's discuss concentrative meditation.

Your goal is a simple one. You will learn to produce a deep state of relaxation in fifteen to twenty minutes, while creating inner peace. You are going to achieve this goal while sitting quietly in a comfortable position, in a relaxing environment, with your eyes closed, while repeating a KEY WORD as you breathe and relax.

I know the idea seems daunting, but it is not.

The beauty of this exercise is its simplicity. All you need to do is breathe, relax and have an open mind for fifteen to twenty minutes. Don't forget, this is not a contest. Your mind will naturally wander during the process, and your goal is to refocus it. To do so, you will repeat the key word. What is a key word? It is a word that elicits a sense of well-being.

A key word is a very personal choice; for me, that word is *peace*. For you, it could be *serenity, love, harmony, tranquility*. It could even be a word that touches on one of the senses: touch, taste, sound, sight or smell. Smell, in fact, is an extremely powerful emotional connector; for some, *cinnamon* might evoke a sense of safety and peace.

It is time to get started. First, you need to pick your key word; remember, it should be a word that evokes something relaxing. Some people prefer a single-syllable word over a multiple-syllable word.

Next, you need to find a quiet, relaxing space, free of external stimuli, a place where you can sit quietly for fifteen to twenty minutes without interruption. It is preferable to sit in a straight-backed chair; however, the sofa or floor will do. Avoid swivel or rocking chairs, though, and the bed. You do not want to get so comfortable that you fall asleep. Turn off all electronics: phones, cell phones, televisions, CD players, etc. As carefully as you try to control your environment, a loud, startling noise can still interrupt you: A dog might bark, a child might scream, a car might backfire outside your window. You will strive to remain calm and breathe through any of these intermittent sounds.

Most people find it difficult to get comfortable after a big meal, so it is best to meditate on an empty stomach or at least an hour after eating.

To begin, close your eyes and concentrate on your breath. Then think of your key word. With each breath, I want you to feel your muscles relaxing, starting from your head and working down to your toes. Relax your forehead, shoulders, chest, hands, abdomen, thighs, feet and toes. Remember to breathe slowly and naturally. Be kind and gentle to yourself.

Your mind will want to wander. That is in the nature of this exercise. Once you close your eyes and focus your attention on your breathing, thoughts and/or images may start to appear. It almost may seem as if you are sitting in a theater watching a play on the stage in front of you. When this happens, remind yourself that you are the audience, not the actor, writer, producer or director. What unfolds and shows itself to you has no intrinsic meaning. These are just images. Do not judge them. Do not berate yourself for not getting the meditation right. Wandering thoughts are absolutely normal; they are the purpose for the key word. Silently repeating the key word to yourself refocuses you back into the present moment.

In the beginning, you will feel as if you are doing nothing but repeating your key word. That, too, is absolutely normal. With time and practice, you will have longer intervals of "peaceful relaxation" before needing to draw on your key word.

Again, this is not a contest. This is about allowing your body and mind to rest. Do not force it. Do not attempt to control your thoughts and emotions; when thoughts and images appear, simply breathe calmly and repeat your key word.

You may use a watch or a clock to check the time; just make sure it does not tick. Gently open your eyes and glance at the clock. If you see you have more time, take a nice deep breath, close your eyes, relax your body and repeat your key word.

Let's get started.

Close your eyes.

Sit quietly in your comfortable clothing. Place your hands on your upper thighs, palms up. Let your shoulders relax and fall.

Concentrate on your breathing. As you inhale and exhale through your nose, silently say your KEY WORD.

An example:

As I INHALE, "PEACE."

As I EXHALE, "PEACE."

Keep your breathing natural and slow. With each breath, allow your body to sink deeper into your seat. Fifteen to twenty minutes is your goal. Given time and practice, you will discover you are not repeating your key word as often as at the beginning. You may open your eyes to check the time, then slowly close them and continue the meditation. When you are finished, keep your eyes closed for a few minutes and sit quietly. Then open your eyes and sit for another few minutes before getting up.

Ultimately, there is no right or wrong way to relax. If, after a few days, you find that you really cannot quiet your mind with concentrative meditation, go down to the nearest self-help bookstore and purchase a guided-meditation CD. There are some wonderful meditation CDs out there.

The goal is to incorporate meditation into your life, once or twice a day. Some people prefer to meditate when they wake up and again before they go to bed. It really does not matter when. Just do it!

Do not give up. Physiological benefits are accruing whether you feel it or not.

Massage, acupuncture and **chiropractic medicine** are other tools that can be utilized as often as possible to alleviate panic and anxiety. All three help encourage alignment, balance and relaxation. As the RESEARCHER, you have learned it is a physical impossibility to experience panic and/or anxiety while you are relaxed. This chapter makes it quite clear what your mission is and gives you all the tools you need.

Now get busy getting relaxed!

Chapter Twelve

SLEEP THE NIGHT AWAY

"The best cure for insomnia is to get a lot of sleep."
—*W.C. Fields*

One of the best defenses against panic and anxiety is to get the proper amount of sleep. On the flip side, one of the quickest ways to create panic and anxiety is sleep deprivation. Without the proper amount of sleep, the brain's ability to think, handle stress, process emotions and solve problems deteriorates. That is why sleep deprivation is one of the first tactics applied to prisoners of war. Anyone who suffers from panic and/or anxiety can understand that very well. The war being waged between your mind and your body is excruciating.

Again, you are not alone in this war: Millions of Americans suffer from long- and short-term sleep disorders associated with panic and anxiety.

Sleep boosts the immune system while recharging the nervous system. Seven to eight hours of quality sleep is what the average adult requires. In order to achieve this, you need to develop what we will call your ritual SLEEP TACTICS.

SLEEP TACTICS
1. Prioritize your to-do list.

Nothing will keep you awake more than thinking about all the things you need to get accomplished the following day. At the end of the day, look over your next day's to-do list, rearrange the items according to how important they are or how soon they need to be done, and break large projects into smaller, more manageable tasks. Create your list before you eat dinner. That way, you will not be focusing on work before you climb into bed.

2. *Develop a relaxing bedtime routine.*

   Turn off your computer, phones, PDA devices and the television thirty minutes before bedtime. These devices do nothing but stimulate the brain! Take a hot shower or bath. Read, listen to some relaxing music or meditate.

3. *Set the thermostat to 68 degrees.*

   If your room is too hot or too cold, you will not sleep well. Sixty-eight degrees is cool enough for you to use a blanket without getting too warm.

4. *Create a womblike atmosphere in your bedroom.*

   Make sure the lighting is low and soft, the drapes and/or blinds are closed, and your mattress, pillows and bed are comfortable.

5. *Avoid caffeine (including chocolate), alcohol and nicotine.*

   You have already learned what these substances do to your body. Contrary to common belief, alcohol will disrupt your sleep, not sedate you. Caffeine is present in your system for eight hours after consumption. Smoking in bed is dangerous.

6. *Avoid eating and drinking before bedtime.*

   You can have a small snack about an hour before bedtime, but nothing spicy, and limit what you drink before bed. It is a good idea to go to the bathroom right before you go to sleep. This will help alleviate the need to use the bathroom in the middle of the night.

7. *Use a fan, air purifier or sound-sleep machine (*not *the television or radio) to block distracting noise.*

    Many people need "white noise" in order to sleep, to block background noise and even, for some, the sound of silence. White noise is sound that creates frequency in equal amounts. Television and radio are not good sources because the music, action, voices and commercials are all geared at different levels and frequencies, which will wake you up!

8. *Exercise, exercise, exercise.*

    At the risk of sounding like a broken record, let me reiterate that exercising every day will help you sleep better. Just make sure to give your body three hours of rest between your workout and bedtime.

9. *Go to bed and wake up at the same time every day.*

    Yes, even on weekends. It will help to reinforce your sleep-wake cycle. That will only happen with consistency.

10. *Limit naps to twenty minutes.*

    Because of your body's circadian rhythms, you will naturally feel an afternoon low between one and four p.m. I used to attribute this to eating a heavy lunch. But after weeks of eating healthily and still feeling that way, I discovered that natural low cycle in our rhythms. Make sure to limit your nap to twenty to thirty minutes, or you could disrupt your evening sleep.

11. *Use the bedroom for sleeping.*

    Do not work, do homework or watch television in bed. If the bedroom is the only place you have a television, you need to turn it off thirty minutes before bedtime.

12. *No ticking clocks!*

   Make sure you have a quiet clock, and once you set the alarm, turn the clock away from you. This way, if you sleep on your side, you will not be looking at the clock or see the time when you open your eyes.

13. *Follow the 20-20 rule.*

   If you cannot fall asleep within twenty minutes, go into another room and sit calmly and quietly. Do not watch television, read a detective novel or surf the Internet. Relax for twenty minutes, but do not fall asleep in this room. Return to your bedroom, and if after twenty minutes, you still can't fall asleep, repeat these steps until you are ready to fall asleep in your bed.

With panic and/or anxiety, it is important to make sleep a top priority. We all know what it feels like when you are stuck in that sleepless nightmare. The good news is that in previous chapters, you have been given some great tools to help you sleep: diet, exercise, yoga, proper breathing, meditation. By combining those tools with your new SLEEP TACTICS, you should be well on your way to getting a good night's sleep!

But if after one week, you are still not sleeping, it is time to do more. You want to rule out any medical conditions before you start taking supplements, over-the-counter sleep aids and/or medication. It is crucial to work closely with your mental health practitioner, who will evaluate your condition before deciding on the appropriate course of action. Dosage, frequency, side effects and medication interactions must be explained to you by a qualified mental health practitioner, not the guy at the health food store!

Do not indiscriminately start self-medicating.

The following supplements, over-the-counter sleep aids and medications are available today. Remember, you are the RESEARCHER. Find out anything and everything you can about these tools, and discuss the pros and cons with your mental health practitioner.

SUPPLEMENTS

Melatonin: This is a hormone produced in the brain by the pineal gland. Research indicates that 0.1 to 0.3 milligrams (mg) should be sufficient for most people. Health food stores sell dosages ten times higher (3 mg), which has been noted to be less effective in treating insomnia and, in fact, may create a hangover effect. Research has also shown that for insomnia, the fast-release melatonin is probably more effective than the slow-release formulas. If you consider taking melatonin, less is more. Start slow.

Valerian: Prepared from the roots of the valerian plant, valerian is used for insomnia and anxiety. While some people feel its effects immediately, research indicates it is generally more effective when taken over longer periods (several weeks). Dosage recommendations are anywhere from 150 mg to 900 mg. As with any of these supplements, there are possible side effects. Again, less is more. Start slow.

5-Hydroxytryptopan (5-HTP): 5-HTP is a naturally occurring amino acid that helps boost the neurotransmitter serotonin. It is also the precursor to melatonin, which helps regulate the sleep cycle. Dosages range from 50 to 300 mg. Take it thirty to forty-five minutes before bedtime.

Chamomile and **passion flower:** Both these herbs have been used as sleeping aids for centuries, although there is no established safe and effective dosage regarding either one. It is best to start at a low dosage and monitor its effectiveness. If it seems to be working but not quite well enough, increase the dosage until it feels right. If you feel groggy or dizzy, lower the dosage. Use your common sense.

Calcium/magnesium: Tension, irritability, muscle cramps and nervousness have been linked to insufficient amounts of calcium and magnesium. You will find these two elements together, in tablets or capsules, because magnesium helps regulate the transport of calcium into the bones and blood. There should be a two-to-one ratio. The higher proportion is given to calcium, since it is harder for the body to absorb; 1,000 mg of calcium to 500 mg of magnesium is advisable. Taking a calcium/magnesium supplement before bedtime each night may help your sleep quality by relaxing the muscles and soothing the nervous system.

And here's an added bonus: These supplements may also help alleviate panic and anxiety.

OVER-THE-COUNTER SLEEP AIDS

Many over-the-counter sleeping medications contain antihistamines, or a combination of antihistamines and a pain reliever. Antihistamines have a sedating quality, which is why many people use them as sleep inducers.

Antihistamines: Nytol, Sleep-Ez,Sominex. Active ingredient: diphenhydramine

Antihistamines With Pain Relievers: Tylenol P.M., Excedrin P.M., Anacin P.M. Active ingredients: acetaminophen and diphenhydramine

Allery Antihistamines: Benadryl. Active ingredient: diphenhydramine hydrochloride

Chlor-Trimeton. Active ingredient: chlorpheniramine

Atarax or Vistaril. Active ingredient: hydroxyzine

All of these over-the-counter sleep aids are inexpensive and readily available. As with most medications, some people may have adverse reactions or experience side effects. So again, it is important to discuss the pros and cons of these sleep aids with your mental health practitioner.

PRESCRIPTION SLEEP AIDS

There have been incredible breakthroughs regarding prescription medications for sleep. In the old days, medium-to- long-acting benzodiazepines (Dalmane, Klonopin, Doral, Halcion, Xanax, Restoril, Serax, Prezepam) were the most commonly prescribed sleep hypnotics. With that group of medications, there was a higher risk of intolerance and dependency. Today we have a class of short-term non-benzodiazepines that can induce sleep with far fewer side effects. They have been created to satisfy a broad spectrum of sleeping issues.

Ambien, Ambien Cr and Lunesta: These medications were created for people who have difficulty falling asleep. Ambien is generic. Ambien CR and Lunesta are not yet generic but have proven to be more effective. There is some discussion that these medications can interfere with your REM cycle, which means you may not feel totally rested when you awake.

Sonata: This is the medication for people who can fall asleep but cannot stay asleep. Sonata is a short-acting medication, meaning the effects will wear off more quickly, so if you wake up at 2 a.m., you can take it without fear of being too groggy in the morning.

Rozerem: This is for someone who has been having sleep issues for a prolonged period of time. Unlike Ambien and Lunesta, Rozerem does not disturb REM sleep. It does not

cause dependence and is the first sleep drug in its class not des-
ignated as a controlled substance.

ANTIDEPRESSANT SLEEP AIDS

Trazadone: Usually administered in low dosages, this
sleep tool is used to treat insomnia that may be caused by
depression, also known as secondary insomnia.

Amitriptyline, Doxepin, Mirtazipine: These are other
antidepressants frequently prescribed to help treat insomnia.

As you can see, a variety of supplements and over-the-
counter, prescription and antidepressant sleep aids are available. Do not be afraid to use these tools if necessary.

I had to learn this lesson the hard way. For six months,
I tortured myself unnecessarily, trying everything short of a
witch doctor to help alleviate my sleep issues. Sleep deprived,
miserable and unable to focus, I finally had to admit to myself
that "my way" was not going to work. Finally, I relinquished
control to the experts. It was the best decision I ever made.

One of the greatest tools against panic and anxiety is getting a good night's sleep. If you do everything outlined in this
book, you should be well on your way to sleeping the night away.

Chapter Thirteen

SUPPLE-MENTAL-ATION

"Life expectancy would grow by leaps and bounds
if green vegetables smelled as good as bacon."
—*Doug Larson*

In the chapter called "Running on Empty," you learned which foods best promote a healthy mind and body. It is important to understand that chronic stress, poor diet and certain medical conditions can deplete the body's stores of vital nutrients, so much so that food alone may be unable to satisfy your body's need for vitamins and minerals. Scientists the world over are busy examining vitamin deficiencies as an underlying contributing factor to panic and/or anxiety.

Below are some vitamins, minerals and herbs that might help with symptoms of panic and/or anxiety. None of them has been approved by the FDA for this purpose. The law clearly states that *if a dietary supplement label includes such a claim [i.e., "This product might help decrease the symptoms of panic and anxiety"], it must state in a "disclaimer" that the FDA has not evaluated this claim. The disclaimer must also state that this product is not intended to "diagnose, treat, cure or prevent any disease," because legally such a claim can be made only for a drug.*

The National Institutes of Health (NIH), U.S. Food and Drug Administration (FDA) and National Agricultural Library (NAL) all have on their websites warnings and extensive information on usage and safety regarding vitamin, mineral and herb supplements.

Many of the vitamins and herbs discussed in the previous chapter are also tools to reduce panic and anxiety. To refresh your memory, they are valerian, 5-HTP, chamomile, passion flower and calcium/magnesium.

The following is a list of vitamins, minerals and herbs that research is showing may help lessen the effects of panic and/ or anxiety.

Vitamin Bs: These include vitamins B1 (thiamine), B2 (riboflavin), B3 (niacin/niacinamide), B5 (pantothenic acid), B6 (pyridoxal phosphate), B8 (inositol), B9 (folic acid) and B12 (cobalimin). The B complex is highly important in influencing physical and mental performance, as well as mental and emotional well-being. Deficiency has been linked to panic, anxiety and insomnia. Since these vitamins cannot be stored in the body, we must rely entirely on our daily diet to supply them.

GABA (Gamma-amino butyric acid): An important inhibitory neurotransmitter regulating the firing of neurons, GABA helps reduce excitability. That, in turn, helps reduce anxiety while inducing relaxation and sleep.

Taurine: This is an amino acid that, like GABA, works as an inhibitory neurotransmitter, calming and stabilizing the brain and central nervous system.

NAC (N-acetylcysteine): A metabolite of the amino acid cysteine, NAC increases levels of glutathione in the brain. A deficiency in glutathione has shown to be linked to depression, panic and anxiety.

L-theanine: The amino acid L-theanine has been shown to induce deep states of relaxation while creating a calming effect. If taken before bedtime, it may promote sleep, which is why it has been called a natural Xanax/Valium alternative.

Selenium: A deficiency in selenium may be associated with increased anxiety, depression and fatigue.

Chromium picolinate: This trace mineral has shown a significant effect on people suffering from atypical depression.

Alpha-linolenic acid: Some research indicates that people who suffer from panic attacks may be deficient in alpha-linolenic acid, which can be found in most seed oils. Examples include flaxseed, walnut, rapeseed (commonly known as canola) and soybean. These oils are high in omega-3 fatty acids and are known to affect the brain's serotonin levels.

These supplements are wonderful tools, and in many cases they work better when taken in an integrated formula. I realize that I have hammered you with many important things to remember, but this is really important: Consult with your mental health practitioner before you add any supplements to your regimen. Used correctly, they can be highly effective tools in breaking yet another link in the panic and/or anxiety chain.

Chapter Fourteen

MEDICATION OR ICE CREAM?

"For peace of mind, resign as general manager of the universe."
—*Author unknown*

I s there any doubt which you would choose if given the option? You would take ice cream over medication any day of the week. For some, however, the decision is not that simple; the Rocky Road has worn us out.

As I have mentioned, my personal journey was a difficult one, especially regarding the medication issue. I grew up in a family that was out of control. Drinking, drugs, smoking, rage, drama, you name it; it was all done to excess. By the time I was five years old, it was clear to me that I had to be in control, because no one else would be. There is no question that this survival technique helped save my life. I have since lost my mother, my father, my younger sister, my aunt and my grandparents to different forms of excess.

In my thirties, with the onset of panic and anxiety, my body and mind seemed to be rebelling against me. I could not understand where it was coming from. All of the horrible experiences were behind me, so none of the panic and anxiety I felt made any sense.

I can remember sitting in my therapist's office and hearing him say, "You don't see it now, but some day this experience will turn out to be one of the best things that has ever happened to you."

I couldn't believe my ears.

I looked him in the eyes and said, "I have survived emotional abuse, physical abuse, sexual abuse; I have been robbed and kidnapped, all before I was twenty! Twelve years later, I am having panic and anxiety. The best thing that has ever happened to me? You have got to be kidding me!

"I don't drink, I don't smoke, I don't do drugs. I have never even had a cup of coffee! Don't I get extra credit? I never caused any trouble; I always did the right thing. I was a good kid!"

That is when the epiphany hit. Panic and anxiety is what happens to the good kids! We always did what we were told, we never acted out and, most of the time, we stuffed our feelings.

But control, that great survival technique that worked so well in my childhood, was now playing me for a fool. I had outgrown my survival technique, yet out of habit I was still gripping onto it for dear life.

For months, I had experienced strange physical sensations, and by the time I ended up in the therapist's chair, I had seen at least ten doctors and had been tested for what seemed to be every disease known to man. All with the same result: There was nothing physically wrong with me. I was told that I had the body of an Olympic athlete. This just underscored the fact that I was indeed going crazy!

Every one of these medical doctors suggested that I was under a lot of stress and attempted to steer me toward medication. There was NO WAY I was going down that road! I grew up watching drugs and alcohol destroy my family. It was not going to happen to me! After surviving everything I had, I just knew that, through sheer will power, I could beat this thing without medication.

My world became smaller and smaller. At the time, I was

six months overdue fulfilling a modeling contract in Japan. I could barely leave my house, let alone get on a plane. My life was falling apart. The sad thing, in retrospect, is that all I had to do was follow the medical advice I had been given.

I learned the hard way that medication exists for a reason. Do not forget this. There is no need to live a life of perpetual fear. It is my greatest wish that the tools I have presented in this book will work for you, and that you will not need any medication. However, if you find that you do need medication, please do not worry yourself sick about taking it.

Antidepressants were originally created and marketed for depression. As time went on, the medical profession discovered that antidepressants also worked for panic and anxiety. While they may be called *drugs* and *medications*, ANTIDEPRESSANTS DO NOTHING BUT AFFECT CHEMICALS THAT ALREADY EXIST IN YOUR BRAIN!

That is correct. Read it again.

ANTIDEPRESSANTS DO NOTHING BUT AFFECT CHEMICALS THAT ALREADY EXIST IN YOUR BRAIN!

Shocking, isn't it?

To explain without getting too technical, a healthy body creates certain chemical messengers (serotonin, dopamine and noradrenalin) that allow communication between your nerve cells. Under stress, your body consumes more of these messengers (serotonin, dopamine and noradrenalin) than it is creating, thus producing what is thought to be a chemical imbalance. The antidepressants prescribed for panic and/or anxiety are designed to step up the availability of these messengers to your brain.

It truly is that simple. You are depleting the chemicals faster than you are creating them.

All of the antidepressants available for panic and/or anxiety target serotonin. The Selective Serotonin Reuptake Inhibitors (SSRI) and the Selective Serotonin-Norepinephrine Reuptake Inhibitors (SNRI) are the preferred antidepressants for panic and/or anxiety, because they have fewer side effects than their older counterparts.

SELECTIVE SEROTONIN REUPTAKE INHIBITORS: These target only the serotonin neurotransmitter. The most common SSRIs are Celexa, Lexapro, Luvox, Paxil, Prozac and Zoloft.

SELECTIVE SEROTONIN-NOREPINEPHRINE REUP-TAKE INHIBITORS: These target both the serotonin and the norepinephrine neurotransmitters. The brand names are Effexor and Cymbalta.

These antidepressant medications are often preferred over traditional anti-panic and anti-anxiety drugs because the risk for dependency and abuse is less. You and your doctor will have to decide, given your medical history and diagnosis, which will best suit your needs. The Recipe for Panic and Anxiety will help you and your doctor understand what is happening in your specific situation and help you choose the appropriate medication if needed.

It is important to understand that your doctor is not a mind reader. He or she is not God. He or she does not live in your body. For this process to work, you must be proactive. Discuss your fears and feelings and **find out what possible side effects to expect.**

The Internet is a wonderful tool for research, but be careful how you interpret the articles and postings regarding these medications. I totally flipped myself out after reading the side effects of the medication my doctor had prescribed.

I immediately called him and told him that, after researching the medication and seeing its side effects, I did not feel comfortable taking *any* medication. By law, a pharmaceutical company must list any "possible side effects" for any given medication. You can find many of those side effects in aspirin and Tylenol.

My doctor was extremely supportive, assuring me that he did not indiscriminately prescribe medications, and that he felt this medication would be very beneficial. He reminded me that it was my decision but said if he were in my shoes, he would have no problem taking the medication he was prescribing.

I realized that what is missing from the bald statements you read on websites is the years of medical school and practice during which physicians learn how to match patient and medication. Their specialized knowledge allows them to know which side effects apply to which patient and what to ignore. My doctor reassured me that he was available on a daily basis, and that if I was feeling uncomfortable or strange, all I had to do was call.

Although it was a difficult decision, I felt that with my doctor's support and understanding, I could take the medication. It generally takes four to eight weeks for an antidepressant to take effect, and while there are possible side effects, they do not normally pose a problem. As the RESEARCHER, you already have learned that with panic and/or anxiety, you are hyperaware of every little change that occurs in your body. The tendency will be to overreact to the first side effect. But you can put your self-talk tools to work. For example, "These are temporary responses." "I know it will take four to eight weeks for this medicine to take effect, but that doesn't mean my body won't be making adjustments daily." "I have discussed these side effects with my doctor, and I am not in danger." "These reactions and responses are temporary."

If it is at all possible during the beginning of the medication process, I recommend making a weekly appointment with your doctor so you can discuss your progress. This will help alleviate your fears and concerns. It will give both of you the reassurance that you are on the right track. The two of you are working as a team, remember, and to be successful you need to have an open, honest relationship. Your doctor is not a mind reader. If you need reassurance, call, email or fax him or her. If you discover that your doctor is unavailable to you, or does not return your phone calls, emails or faxes in a timely manner, you need to find another doctor.

If, after six weeks, you do not feel significantly better, you and your doctor should discuss the possibility of switching to another medication. Do not stop until you find the right one. Too many people end up on the wrong medication because they did not speak up. You cannot blame your doctor for this. And feeling "okay" is not good enough. I cannot stress this too strongly. You do not want to wake up ten years from now still feeling "okay." Keep trying, and be patient. The right antidepressant is out there, and there are other, alternative medications as well.

Under certain circumstances and for a short time, your doctor may prescribe a benzodiazepine (Xanax, Ativan, Klonopin) or a beta blocker (Inderal, Tenormin) in conjunction with your antidepressant. This approach will give you some relief until the antidepressant takes effect. The thing to remember about these medications is that they are designed to do one thing and one thing only: relax you!

As I have gone to great pains to inform you, it is a physical impossibility to have panic and/or anxiety if you are relaxed. Your goal, of course, is to try to achieve this without medication. If, however, you are still in a place of panic and/or anxiety after trying the relaxation techniques discussed in this book, be gentle and kind to yourself. Do not beat yourself up. Take the medication. Your body requires rest in order to mend and heal.

These medications are designed to relieve your panic and/or anxiety, but they should not be thought of as a cure. They do not treat the underlying cause of the panic or anxiety disorder. Working closely with your mental health practitioner will help you get to the root of the problem and develop better coping skills. Once you replace panic and anxiety with your two new best friends, RELAXATION AND SLEEP, you will rediscover that anything and everything is possible. Have confidence that together, you and your doctor will work this out.

Chapter Fifteen

THE BIGGER PICTURE

"Experience is not what happens to a man, it is what a man does with what happens to him."
—Aldous Huxley

When I look back at the progression of my panic and anxiety, I realize that at the onset of my journey, I was asking myself big questions. I was at a crossroads in my working life, my personal life and my creative life. I had been driving myself for years; I had never taken the time to stop and smell the roses. I had been operating on the assumption that financial freedom would make me happy and set me free. That the perfect person—someone who would make me happy, mend my wounds and save me—was somewhere out there waiting to set me free. That my creativity would make me happy and bring me fame and fortune. And yet, there I was: miserable, alone and shaking in my shoes with unbearable panic and anxiety.

I remember thinking, "How did I get here?"

Then I asked myself the three most important questions of my life: "What is it all for?" "Is this all there is?" "What is my true purpose?" I can honestly tell you that that day was the day I started living my life.

Soon thereafter, I learned to simplify my goals. As long as I had enough money to pay my bills and have food on the table, I was thankful. The reality regarding money is simple: You will never see a Brinks truck following a hearse. By that, I mean you cannot take any of that money or those things you acquired to the grave. So why are they so damned important? Let us hope that when it is our time, the one thing we do take with us is the knowledge we have gained along the way, so the next time around, we can learn a whole new set of lessons.

Regarding relationships, when I see Humpty Dumpty, I now shove Humpty Dumpty over the wall. I no longer need to fix or make anyone into the incredible person I think he or she should be in order to save me. The product either comes fully assembled or I do not purchase it. I no longer need anyone to save me; I have the tools to save myself.

I can tell you this about creativity: It is the most powerful tool in the world. Nothing and no one can take it away from you. Nurture it, protect it and, by all means, use it to create good in this world.

We all have a choice in life. We either choose to be present or we choose to be a victim of the future or the past. Jobs, relationships, family and friends will come and go. You and I, however, will not. No one lives in our brains except us. Nurture, love and support your thoughts; as I've said before, you have exceptional talents in this area.

I will leave you with a final mantra:

Today I will nurture and cherish the relationship I have with myself. I will live this day, the only day I truly know I have, to the best of my ability, treating myself, and everyone who crosses my path, with dignity, integrity and compassion. I will learn and experience as much of life as I can, while remembering to smile, and not taking the challenges life throws at me so damned seriously.

And when I put my head on that pillow tonight, I will have no regrets. If I wake up tomorrow, I will take a moment to be thankful, reminding myself that this body I reside in is truly one of the most miraculous gifts in the world. I will honor it, protect it and nurture it as long as I shall live.

I would be lying if I told you this panic and anxiety journey has been at all an easy one. However, by being open and sharing my story with friends, acquaintances and strangers, I discovered, somewhere along the path, the true purpose of my life. It is about giving. It is about understanding that each of us has the ability to affect many lives. It is my sincere hope that, through my journey, I have somehow made your journey easier.

PANIC & ANXIETY RECIPE

Serves: 1
Preheat Brain to: Past or Future
*Although there are many recipes for Panic and Anxiety, the main
ingredients are universal. Check all that apply so that you can share
this recipe with your mental health practitioner.*

INGREDIENTS:	YES	NO
Avoiding People	❏	❏
Avoiding Places	❏	❏
Avoiding Things	❏	❏
Being Easily Distracted	❏	❏
Blurred Vision	❏	❏
Chest pains	❏	❏
Chills	❏	❏
Diarrhea	❏	❏
Difficulty Concentrating	❏	❏
Dizziness	❏	❏
Dry Mouth	❏	❏
Eye Twitching, Clenched Jaws, Teeth Grinding	❏	❏
Excess Sweating	❏	❏
Excess Worry about your health	❏	❏
Fatigue	❏	❏
Feelings of Unreality	❏	❏
Fear of Being Institutionalized	❏	❏
Fear of Crowds, Confined & Public Places	❏	❏
Fear of Dying	❏	❏
Fear of Eating in front of others	❏	❏
Fear of Going Crazy	❏	❏
Fear of Leaving a Familiar Place	❏	❏
Fear of Losing Control	❏	❏
Fear of Social Events	❏	❏
Fear of Speaking in Front of Others	❏	❏
Fear of Traveling Alone in a Plane, Car, Train, etc...	❏	❏
Fever	❏	❏
Feeling on Edge	❏	❏
Feeling a Lump in your Throat	❏	❏
Headache	❏	❏

	YES	NO
Hot Flashes	❏	❏
Hyperventilating	❏	❏
Irritability	❏	❏
Impatience	❏	❏
Loss of Feelings in Hands or Feet	❏	❏
Muscle Tension, Tightness or Achiness	❏	❏
Nausea	❏	❏
Numbness or Tingling Sensations	❏	❏
Rapid, Pounding Heartbeat	❏	❏
Restlessness	❏	❏
Shaking	❏	❏
Shortness of breath	❏	❏
Stomachache	❏	❏
Sudden, Intense Feelings of Fear and or Doom	❏	❏
Tightness in your Chest	❏	❏
Trouble Falling or Staying Asleep	❏	❏
Worry about what Others Think	❏	❏

HAVE YOU FOUND YOURSELF THINKING:

	YES	NO
I am going crazy	❏	❏
I am going to die	❏	❏
I am going to make a fool of myself	❏	❏
I am having a heart attack	❏	❏
I am trapped	❏	❏
I can't be alone	❏	❏
I can't catch my breath	❏	❏
I could faint or pass out	❏	❏
I could lose control	❏	❏
I have a brain tumor	❏	❏

ARE YOU FEELING:

	YES	NO
Angry	❏	❏
Criticized	❏	❏
Depressed	❏	❏
Embarrassed	❏	❏
Isolated	❏	❏
Lonely	❏	❏
Trapped	❏	❏

And here you thought you were all alone!

ACKNOWLEDGMENTS

I could not have accomplished any of this without my family of friends. Anyone who has survived panic and/or anxiety knows this to be true. Thank you to Nancy and John for always being there and for teaching me the true meaning of *family*. I would not be the person I am today without the love and support from Godeane, aka Mother Earth.

I count my blessings when it comes to the experts who have crossed my path. Rick Shuman, PhD, one of the best psychologists Los Angeles has to offer. Dr. Robert Gerner, the most patient man in the world and a wizard of psychopharmacology and psychiatry. Dr. David Allen, who taught me that Eastern medicine is just as good as, and sometimes better than, the Western approach. Dr. Michele Craske, the first doctor who helped me make sense of all the books and literature I had read on panic and anxiety.

Most of all, I would like to thank my family. I took every wonderful quality you possessed and chose to understand and forgive the pain of the others. Without the good and the bad experiences, this book would never have been written.

This would not be a proper acknowledgment if I did not thank Wikipedia® (a registered trademark of the Wikimedia Foundation, Inc.) for being the best online dictionary resource in the world!

If not for the support and guidance of Amy Rennert, the eagle eye of Pamela Feinsilber, and the creative wonder of Dorothy Smith, this book would not exist.

A special thanks to the incredible Lin Dobbs-Shannon for reminding me that less is (so much) more.

RESOURCE LIST

NATIONAL INSTITUTE OF MENTAL HEALTH
Science Writing, Press and Dissemination Branch
6001 Executive Boulevard
Room 8184, MSC 9663
Bethesda, MD 20892-9663
1-866-615-6464 (toll-free)
www.nimh.nih.gov

ANXIETY DISORDERS ASSOCIATION OF AMERICA
8730 Georgia Avenue
Suite 600
Silver Springs, MD 20910
1-240-485-1001
www.adaa.org

AMERICAN PSYCHIATRIC ASSOCIATION
1000 Wilson Boulevard
Suite 1825
Arlington, VA 22209
1-888-35-PSYCH (toll-free)
From outside the U.S. and Canada, 1-703-907-7300
Email: apa@psych.org

AMERICAN PSYCHOLOGICAL ASSOCIATION
750 First Street, NE
Washington, DC 20002-4242
1-800-374-2721 (toll-free) or 1-202-336-5500
www.apa.org

INTERNET RESOURCES
- www.foodsafety.gov/~dms/supplmnt.html
- http://dietary-supplements.info.nih.gov/health_information/health_information.aspx
- http://fnic.nal.usda.gov/nal_display/index.php?info_center=4&tax_level=1&tax_subject=274
- www.recovery-inc.org
- http://www.ocfoundation.org

"Panic and/or Anxiety research constantly evolves so feel free to visit us at **www.SnapOutOfIt.tv** for up-to-date research regarding science, supplements and medication."

— NOTES —

— NOTES —

— NOTES —

— NOTES —

— NOTES —

— NOTES —

— NOTES —

— NOTES —

— NOTES —

— NOTES —

— NOTES —

— NOTES —

— NOTES —

— NOTES —

— NOTES —

— NOTES —

— NOTES —

— NOTES —

— NOTES —

— NOTES —

— NOTES —

— NOTES —

Made in the USA
Lexington, KY
18 February 2011